A Puncher's Chance

Jeff Weddle

RUST BELT PRESS
BUFFALO, NY

Grateful acknowledgment is made to the following, where some of these pieces have been accepted for publication or previously appeared, sometimes in slightly different form: *Alien Buddha Press*, *Alien Buddha Wears a Yellow Vest*, *Alien Buddha Zine*, *Blue's Cruzio Café*, *Chiron Review*, *Concrete Mist Anthology 2019*, *Dog River Review*, *Gypsy Art Show*, *Hawai'i Review*, *Heavy Bear*, *Hello Poetry*, *The Imploding Tie-Dyed Toupee*, *Malcontent*, *Open Unison Stop*, *Poetry Feast*, *Pressure Press Presents*, *Protea Poetry Journal*, *Raw Art Review*, *Rust Belt Press*, *Rust Belt Review*, *Slipstream*, and *Wingnut Brigade*.

ISBN 978-0-578-21837-3

Library of Congress Control number 2019936618

Also by Jeff Weddle

Citizen Relent (Unlikely Books, 2019)

It's Colder than Hell / Starving Elves Eat Reindeer Meat / Santa Claus is Dead (Alien Buddha Press, 2018)

Heart of the Broken World (Nixes Mate Books, 2017)

Comes to This (Nixes Mate Books, 2017)

When Giraffes Flew (Southern Yellow Pine, 2015)

The Librarian's Guide to Negotiation: Winning Strategies for the Digital Age (co-author; Information Today, 2012)

Betray the Invisible (OEOCO, 2012)

Bohemian New Orleans: The Story of the Outsider and Loujon Press (University Press of Mississippi, 2007)

Always for Jill

~ Contents ~

A Puncher's
Chance

THE BATTLER

The son of a bitch could hit
no need to tell me.
My face didn't always look like this
but I don't hold no grudges
and I gave as good as I got every damn time.

Most say I was robbed the second fight
the judges maybe in the promoter's pocket
but all we could do was battle till the last bell
and when it was over we went to Dugan's for pints
and the son of a bitch raised my arm
right there in front of all the boys
and all I could do was laugh about it.

But he could hit
don't think he couldn't.
He hit like a hammer.
He might as well have been in it for murder
but that's the way you have to do
if you're gonna last a round.

I'm going to see him tomorrow

leave flowers by the stone.

It's hard to know what to say
hard to know how a man like that can die.

LUCY'S GLORY DAYS

She was fishy, like a flapper
out of bathtub gin.
Got left at the five and dime
with only pennies.

But marks are easy
if you know the right play
and she did.

Everything rattled
where she was.
That was the problem.

No one knew the cause.

Life tasted better when the years
were lighter on her skin,
there was no doubt.

But there was still time to kill.

She slipped a harmonica

into her purse
and found a corner
to put out the hat.

She couldn't play music,
just blew out the stars in her head.
By dinner time
she had eight dollars
and a new lover with a limp.

Six months later
she was working
at a convenience store
in Birmingham
and couldn't remember
his name.

The sunsets were pretty there
and in a town like that
the next man she left behind
just might stay dead.

THAT CONVERSATION

Take this sugar bowl, for example. I don't know where it came from. None of us do. She used it every day and it was always on the table, right in the center, situated on the big rose Jerry thought looked like a red cabbage. That's the way Jerry's mind worked. He saw things in things but didn't understand what was right in front of him. I used to think that's why they got along so well, but who can say? He once told me the rose looked like a cabbage surprised that it was really a rose. He could have been talking about her, you know? God knows she never quite knew her purpose. I think it made her sad, but I also think she took delight in confusion. But take the sugar bowl. No, not as an example. I don't need it. No one here uses sugar anymore.

SECRET IDENTITY QUERY

Maybe you are God
or the next best thing
a leaf falling on a bird
or a cat clawing for love.

Maybe you
are the adversary of light
begging salvation
or maybe you are dead
and don't know it
or you never lived
or haven't yet

and maybe love is a fable
told to children

and maybe
another day will pass
and still nothing
will ever matter

and maybe we

will bid the world
goodnight
and the stars
will do their best
to remain

but I hope
you are the cat
purring now in my lap
as the clock ticks
like mad
as the clock ticks
like mad
as the clock ticks and ticks and ticks
like mad.

BREAKTHROUGH

The epiphany came
and it was this:
I am a word whore.
Easy. Cheap.
This epiphany is not
happy enlightenment.
Being a whore
isn't bad,
but it's not anything
to brag about.
I do not discriminate,
but will wallow and grunt
with most any phrase
that saunters into my head
with an enticing rhythm
or the promise
of some unremarkable reward.
I don't even get money
on the dresser
or a sad dinner.
Word whores rate low
on the scales of prostitution.

But come see me
some fine night.
I'll show you a good time
or at least the best time I can.
All I want is your love
after all
and I'm always around.

THE NEXT BOHEMIANS

unknown poets

in small rooms

apartment houses

not yet built

some will be beautiful

with chewed nails

on delicate fingers

wild hair filled with magic

darting black eyes

and they will know

the same stars

in the same black sky

with everything left

to be written

by them

and all who

come after

when they have

become dust

as did we

long since

and forgotten

PASCAL, UNREMEMBERED

One never hears of Pascal Covici
or the lost conversations of
forgotten writers.
One never considers the thoughts
of lonely mail carriers
or why cats know the fates
of wicked children.
One never thinks of Pascal Covici
in the manner of common thought
or drinks sunlight, pure and golden,
on the dwindling doorstep of time.
One never goes down the garden path
with Pascal Covici dead in the ground.
One simply takes tea and waits.
Pascal Covici could not care less.

AGNES VON KUROWSKY

Of course she was a librarian
before she was a nurse
before she met the young man
whose heart she broke
with a letter.

1919 was languid after all
and one did such things
from a distance.

Of course she was a librarian
who cast aside books
for a life of adventure
a sideways glance
at what the young man
would do in the unfathomed future.

The universe is funny that way
and librarians are no more
necessary than nurses
but this one stumbled
into the glare of genius

and became as the books
on all of our shelves
half-known and beautiful
occasionally caressed
and unimaginably desired.

HEADING DOWN THE HIGHWAY

Windows down and sweating
at eighty miles an hour
Danny Vera turned up loud
the whole world
working in my bones
as the big questions pound hard
about who I can save
who I can kill
and who I can count on.

My answers
like most everybody's
are mostly no one.

Eighty miles an hour
blistering Danny Vera
pounding in my head.

This road belongs to me
straight to the horizon
my ride tuned to
everything in my heart

and like the laughing sun
in the empty sky
and everything I call my own
burning burning burning.

THE SHOW GOES ON

I need to go to the store
and it is freezing outside,
so I fish around in the closet
and find a coat
I've not worn in forever
and slip it on
and put my hands
in the pockets
and find tickets
from a movie I can't place.

It has been so many years
since I wore this jacket
that I can't even remember
the last time I had it on.

But suddenly I get a flash
of your perfume
that hits so hard
I can barely breathe
and I have to sit down

on the couch
and then not even move.

Maybe later I can get back
to what I was doing.

Milk and cereal
and whatever the hell
I thought I needed
can wait.

ORDINARY

What passes for silence
and the children in school
maybe safe.

All we can do is hope.

No television and the cat is in hiding
while the dog naps on Gus's bed
the dishwasher hums in the kitchen
and Jill sleeps upstairs.

The world spins so fast
and a hundred years from now
almost no one drawing breath today
will still be alive

but right this moment
I am trying to hold on
just as you are.

Right this moment
I am here.

ALL THE NOTES

If you're
smart
you learn
every good
story
is about
the girl
made of
music
even if
you never can
get it down.

THE COLLECTOR OF BEAUTIFUL THINGS

The collector of beautiful things
shakes his fists like a man
who knows a large, unpleasant truth
and his walk resembles that of an animal
suffering a painful affliction.
He stares at vistas
no one can quite make out
and mutters iambic pentameter curses
at small children.
The collector of beautiful things
was once thought of as handsome
by those who consider
such things consequential
but "once" is the important word here.
The collector of beautiful things
lives near you.
I cannot say exactly where
though he is outside your window
one night out of ten
and imagines he knows you
better than you know yourself.

He whispers "Sweet dreams"
and means it
for he finds you beautiful
and knows the perfect spot
for your display.
The collector of beautiful things
says hello to you each afternoon
and sometimes you nod
in his direction.
It is all very proper.
I advise you
beautiful one
to put this
out of your mind.
There is nothing you can do
to change what will be.

MAYBE YOU

The last
sentient being
in the universe
unaware of
how alone
it truly was
sat in the ruins
of a dead
forgotten city
staring at
the stars
wondering what
was out there
and dreaming
all the dreams
of happiness.

NATURALLY

A rainy day and desperate
to hear Gilbert O'Sullivan sing
something sad

or somebody say something to thrill me awake
or whatever.

Puddles on the road and wet shoes
Rainy rainy rainy day.

ONCE UPON

The high magic of place
like barber shops
on town squares
old men with their
smudged stories
immortal dogs
and boys
who can sometimes fly.

The high magic of names
and trains in stations
that were busy long ago.

Everything was real
or will be someday.

Give me a bowler hat
and walking stick
and maybe I will change
the world.

ADVICE TO TAKE OR LEAVE

Stay with the task
and you will be
thrice blessed
and these blessings
can be named:
They are peace
and silence
and solitude.

Stay with the task
even if you believe
yourself weak.

You are vast
and the body of miracle
and the strongest person
doing the hardest thing
the thing that must be done.

Stay with the task
until you are finished
until you are taken by light.

Stay with it
as you drink your coffee
as you skin your knees
as your heart continues
as your children grow
as you breathe the living air.

No one will understand
and you will be a hidden god
bending glory
in a dark room

but stay with the task
it is the only way home.

FEDELE TEMPERINI OF
MONTALCINO, TUSCANY

Accident of place
cost you everything, Fedele,
on the spot that mattered
that certain moment
along the Piave at Fossalta.

Maybe you were you there
for cigarettes or candy
or running for
somewhere else
because the battle
asked of you
a different
forgotten valor
along the Piave at Fossalta.

Or maybe you had stopped
to catch your breath
or scream
be silent

or pray
along the Piave at Fossalta.

I hope the mortar claimed you
all at once, Fedele,
while the young American
who lived
took what shrapnel remained
July 8, 1918
along the Piave at Fossalta.

MUSICAL INTERLUDE

I bought two
Rickie Lee Jones
albums for my phone
and went out
into the sunlight
where today
all is permitted
and I love the world
and I bought a bottle of gin
and a cape
and thought of kissing
all the pretty girls
because all is
permitted today
and maybe the world
loves me a little too
and I bought a bucket of dreams
for a dollar and thirty cents
and spilled them into the sky
and somewhere
Rickie Lee is probably
sitting by a pool

outside a large

and beautiful house

and maybe by a quirk of fate

she is reading a poem

I wrote once upon a time

but probably she isn't

and that's fine

because you

are reading this one

right now

and that's plenty

for a guy like me

gin

cape

and everything

practically happy and dancing

under a sky

full of cheap and floating

dreams

MY TRIBE

If your instincts are good
you will choose Hemingway
with his diamond sentences
laid together like brush strokes
from Cezanne.
You will avoid Faulkner's mush.
If your instincts are good
you will choose the woman
who has gifts of her own to share
while also loving yours.
You will avoid the merely beautiful.
If your instincts are good
you will find a way
into the most necessary art
from the commonplace.
You will avoid contrivance.
If your instincts are good
you know these things now.
Otherwise, you will
never understand.
There is no other lesson.

ANAGRAM

One night I dream I'm walking to Hell with a beautiful
young blonde. She is my friend or I love her or both. It's
one of those dreams where much has already happened,
and in great detail, the kind of dream where I feel more
than alive, but all of that is lost, and I have only flashes of
phantasma, a certainty that whatever led us to this walk
along a quiet, dark street, just a regular street, maybe
through a park, with trees around us and lights from
random buildings in the distance, and from normal
streetlights, was quite a story. We are being led on this
ordinary walk to Hell by an attractive, less-obvious brunette
in a long dark coat. She looks like a well-to-do
businesswoman, slightly vamped for a night on the town.
The brunette is in charge of the blonde and me, but she
seems okay, not particularly threatening, just our keeper,
maybe. Maybe our guide. But she has us and we are hers.
At home, there are demons in the walls, but they are more
or less under control. The blonde has short hair and a short
skirt and hot, nerdy glasses and becomes upset at the idea
of sharing her carefully constructed and powerful sex-self
with just anyone, and in the dream I think she means the
people in Hell. The next night I'm on a boat and the end of

the world is coming. Some of us are becoming God and, for a while, can manifest telekinetic powers. The word "heudris" is terribly important, so important that I spell it out in my dream. Later, I look it up. There's no such word, but it is an anagram for Rushdie. These are the Satanic Verses of my dreams.

THE NECESSARY SEARCH

Find a book
of crumbling pages
and fading type
a book with a cracked spine
and odd, unidentifiable stains
scattered among the
dog-eared chapters.
Maybe it has a rip
across the back cover
and holds wonders
lost stories
secret codes
and real danger.
Maybe it is the last copy
of a forgotten edition
by a writer
of no one ever knew
and a publisher
who failed long ago.
Find a book hidden away
in a dead man's attic
or with the discarded effects

of an old woman who once had

a fierce and lovely grace.

Find a book

and bring it to light

a book waiting in the darkness

a book for wise children

the mad

and the lost

a single book

to hold the world

in its embrace

maybe save one soul

a book all but gone

to set you and me

and those who are ready

on fire.

WITH APOLOGIES TO E.E. CUMMINGS

Charles Bukowski's
defunct
    who used to
       ride a whiskeysmooth-black
  Underwood
and write ontwothreeforfive
poemsjustlikethat

      Jesus

he was a homely man
               and what I want
   to know is
how do you like your green-eyed boy
Missus Death

SHARP GUY

and if you're lucky
some woman
somewhere
might have a tattered soul
to patch your pummeled one
in the waltz
between drinks
and betrayal
and you walk on
stealing glances at strangers
just so and dangerous
gliding in your sharp fedora
looking for her everywhere

ZELDA BOLDEN, CIRCUS GIRL

That girl, Zelda, she's a pistol.
Ran off and joined the circus
just like she said she would.
I hear tell she married
some trick shot artist
and does three shows
a night with him.
That girl, Zelda,
she's a beauty, all right.
Someday, she'll be famous.
Count on it.
That girl, Zelda,
she's been breaking hearts
since she's been in skirts.
I should know.
She broke mine in two
when we were 15 years old
and I like to never recovered.
That girl, Zelda, she's a traveler.
She'll ride on forever.
The circus is life and Zelda,

she's the brightest star they've got.

Someday, everyone will know.

THESE MOST PRESSING THINGS

It is easy to give in:
The poverty of the aged
youth with slender chance
lost love, or no love, or love unrequited
hatred become fashion
reason stuffed in a box to die
addled men
women consumed with rage
children left in ovens
starving dogs in the road
cats plotting our death
overpriced dreams
and nightmares ten for a dollar.

It is easy to give in, and if you don't
you will be punished,
but your scars will bear glory.

Your wounds will comfort the infirm.
Your weariness will shine on the darkest night,
the night foretold as the end of things,
and the world might blossom anew.

Or maybe not.

Maybe you will simply resist

and no one but you will know.

Either way, it is agony.

Either way you will be misunderstood.

Reviled.

Either way, to someone, you become the villain.

It is easy to give in.

So many do it every day.

THE BEST ADVICE YOU'LL EVER GET

Work hard at your grades
and get that swell job.

Marry a nice girl and provide for her
like a real man.

Buy a new car and keep it waxed.
Change the oil like clockwork.

Bring children into the world
and wrap them in warm blankets
feed them well
and send them off to school
with fresh eyes and clean clothing.

Likewise feed your dogs and cats
nutritious portions
and if you keep fish
feed them just enough but no more
because fish will kill themselves
with eating.

Kiss your wife when she will allow it.

Attend church regularly
and pray at the recommended times
in the recommended ways.

Go to your job
and avoid trembling or
staring into space for too long
when others are watching.

Brush your hair and teeth.
Bathe regularly.

Do not drink liquor
on public benches
or walk nighttime sidewalks
muttering ancient questions.

Do not read the sages.

Do not give the powers
reason to notice you

unless you are ready
to kick in the bones of the world.

And if you are ready
truly ready
for the blood of ages
to gush where it will
do that instead.

Do it like an axe through bone
unceasing and pure.

Do it like you know
you are a hurricane
or Christ
always ready to kill or die.

SHOWTIME

Consider this cat
sitting quiet
and still
on the arm
of my couch
while the television
plays a film
about a poet
and the trees
in the backyard
present their leaves
to the slow wind.

The cat stares
at something
I cannot name
as the movie poet
enters a bar
and has existential
conversations
over beers
with odd characters

and the leaves
on the backyard trees
dance
if you watch them closely
and the cat blinks once,
yawns
and turns her face to me.

Consider this cat
as the poet in the movie
goes about his business
and I sit here
watching the cat

and the day puddles over
as the cat turns her back
and the whole world
becomes complete
and like everything else
refuses to stop.

PURITY

The simple line
uncluttered
you see it always
with the great ones
Ali's jab
and Hemingway's sentences
and the Golden Gate Bridge
the horizon
and the path between stars
the simple uncluttered line
of a side thrust kick
and Carver's sentences
and Bukowski's
or a tree reaching for the sun
and one heart
calling to another
and the way death takes us
when everything is finished.

THE KNOWN UNIVERSE

Hold the brush. Transmit.

Grey. Red. Magenta.

Beautiful word, magenta.

Of course, there are other colors.

Add and peel away.

Some art requires a needle.

Green. Yellow.

Some art requires a knife.

Hold the brush. Breathe.

Hard then soft. White.

There are shapes which are possible

and shapes which can only be implied.

I was better before.

Blue. Underwater. Blue.

Hold the brush.

Black lines cover and separate.

Transmit. Beautiful word.

All colors masquerade as gold.

THIS IS WHAT I MEANT TO SAY

walk barefoot on glass
black paint and yellow and red
dabbed from a small white bowl
fresh canvas is necessary
like clean brushes and turpentine
walk barefoot on stone
the elements constitute themselves
as air and water
breathe while you are able
and capture light the way angels do
walk barefoot on coals
everything worth having
is blood and fire
walk barefoot in the storm
you are foretold
and death cannot touch you

AUTHOR BIO

Before I was a hobgoblin I was a man
and before that a sparrow
and a cricket
and on down until I was mostly mud.
Pretty much same as you.
And after I was a hobgoblin
I became the air
and loved the sparrows better than other birds.
And after that I became a man again.
That was so long ago and much has changed.
Nothing remains in memory
but shades of blue and gold.
All that was real is ash.

TO BE A KING

Jesus is free, give them all they want.
They will worship you
because Jesus is hate
and hate is everything.
Tell them they can pray anywhere
and beat up queers.
Tell them they can speak in tongues.
Tell them the bad Mexicans
are going back to Mexico
and then straight to Hell,
but Jesus will take care
of good white Americans.
Rape and kill and steal all you want.
Grab some pussy.
Jesus won't give a shit.
Jesus doesn't cost a dime.
Give them all the Jesus they can handle,
then give them some more.
That's how you do it.
Say amen, somebody.

KOWIT THE POET

I have no idea
if that rhymes
but what the hell
today's his birthday
even though
he's dead.

Kowit the poet.

Could that be
why he started
writing in the first place?

Damned shame he died.

The man sent me
free copies of his books
just because
I wrote to say
I liked his work.

Kowit the poet.

Happy birthday
and enjoy
eternity
you dead bastard.

I really did like
your work
and, yes,
all these decades later
I still do.

I HATE MATH

The square root
of a broken heart
cannot be calculated
to the final digit.
Theory describes
the solution
as an infinite string
of non-sequential memories
imperfectly expressed
by the cosine
of irrational desire.
Fuzzy math is a killer
for the bereft.
Only the desperate
would even try.

PAPER DOLL

Maybe I am your shadow
and love poems are so much dust
beneath your maiden aunt's
faded blue rug
the one she bought
for company
twelve years ago
a mistake
she has yet
to grasp
but beautiful in its way
as she herself
once was.

FOR WHAT IT'S WORTH

Write before you know how to write
and believe in yourself
even as you admit in your secret heart
that what you write
is unquestionably bad
awful really
abominable stuff
because
even so
these writings
bad as they are
these writings are of great worth.
They are your education
and bitter work
they are your best and only teachers.
Of course it is important to read
with breadth and discipline
only an imbecile would deny this
but do not put off your own writing
while worshipping
at the feet of the masters.
Read their light

as you pour out your own horrid slop
and if you have to choose
choose writing
and do the best you can.
Someday the scales
will begin to balance
and maybe someday
they will tilt in your favor
but it doesn't much matter.
What matters
is your honest hard effort
to get it down
to find your voice
to find your own true heart
to get it down.

ESKIMO NAPTIME

I wake her at 7:30.
She's lying there
wrapped in her blankets
like an Eskimo
inside a cotton-polyester blend igloo.

"You woke me up several times,"
she complains,
"banging around."

I swear to her
I was asleep
and I am telling the truth
as best I know it,
but she insists....

I must have been
banging around
in my dreams,
dancing with polar bears
way up in her
private arctic circle.

YES

Each day is a lost book
from a secret bible
better than Paris
like kissing a stranger
beneath a bridge
at 10 past midnight
a hand on your cheek
then goodbye.

I HOPE YOU DO

Do you remember
the best poem
the one you knew
before waking
the one shooting
through your skin
electric and dancing
in the vast hollow
between life and no life
understanding the mystery
connections of flow and joy?
Do you remember the poem
you wrote in dreams?

BEAT NIGHT

Small apartment stifled
by dead prose
and blank windows
trampled poets
open to starry night confessions
girls show up
but no one knows what to do
suddenly beer and weed
a party erupts from nothing
most everyone ends broken
sick and tender hearted
one or two are happy
for a while.

THAT POEM

I already wrote that poem
the one that reveals
a saving truth
a truth only you can know
and only know with me
the poem that might actually
save us.

I wrote that poem
sitting in the kitchen
waiting for my coffee to brew
and the cat staring at me
from across the table.

I already wrote that poem
ages ago
I'm sure of it
but did not share it with you
or anybody

and now every word
is lost and forgotten

if in fact I ever wrote them
which as I have said
here and elsewhere
to you and to the cat
I most certainly did.

MAYBE BY HER HAND

The photograph
with your notice
has only your face
your smile and bright eyes

though there was a dog cropped out
a dog with a cone around its neck
and the dog was looking at you
as you smiled
into the camera.

I suppose the dog was yours
and probably wonders
where you have gone
with your tattoos
and the soldier you married

the soldier
who somehow vanished
into doggish dreams.

And I imagine the dog

knows something
beautiful one
of love gone wrong
or maybe something
of other wounds
we are left to imagine
unseen in those bright eyes.

And that is as close
as we can get
to an answer.

ADVICE TO YOU AND THE WIND
AND THE LOST MAIDENS
OF CONSTANTINOPLE

This is the last poem you'll ever need
the perfect ending
to thousands of years of piss
and scribbling
the last poem
you'll ever have to lug around
or suffer as it wraps itself
around your legs
purring like crazy.

This is the last scream from the weeds
the final defeat of art
or maybe a victory.

Everything depends on where you stand
but this is definitely the end of all of it
the last poem of the world
the smudged fingerprint of God
the girl in the black gown
and rapt anticipation.

This is where we came in
and you don't have to go home
but you can't stay here.

It's too late for all of that anyway.

Repeat after me
and find a way to bellow
the last poem
anyone will ever know
the last poem
of the last twinkling night.

Then in the name of love
repeat it all
repeat the poem
and repeat one last time the echo

of the forlorn
and adequate
silence.

ART FINDS ITS WAY

These are the freaks of the earth
and blessed among the human tribe
and come with their portents
to soften the beatings of the unlearned

these few who are cursed
to let the world inside
and shelter it with sorrow

they who tell every true thing
and make up the rest

they whom you loudly ignore
but love in your secret heart

they who are the Judas goats

they who are the pariah's lamp
in the killing darkness

these are the freaks of the earth
and blessed among the human tribe

the carnival barkers and hucksters
the con artists
the needy
the impure saints
the knife fighters in church
the apes of heaven
the drunk children in your basement
the mistakes best forgotten
the wounds of phony Christs
the half-drunk bottles of cut rate vodka
the ashtrays full of death.

They are your dark closets
and your dim beacon.

They allow your shame without penalty.

They are your unknown family

these freaks of the earth
these blessed among the human tribe.

FAT JESUS

Fat Jesus got that way eating the prayers we sent him.
All sugary, empty calories of lip-smacking despair,
the prayers wafted up to Fat Jesus
—that's what the angels started calling him after he
chunked up—
and he couldn't help Himself.
Slurp, slurp, slurp.
Down went the prayers and out came the replies:
holy farts for the most part,
with every ten billionth or so
bringing a happy outcome to the poor,
beaten soul making the request.
Fat Jesus couldn't help it
if most of the prayers he granted
were for small things:
"Dear Jesus, I wish I could find the TV remote."
"Sweet Lord, why won't that bitch drive
just a little bit faster?"
"Heavenly father, please make my mother love me."
Well, that last one usually didn't pan out,
but the others Fat Jesus just did an awesome job with,
whenever the spirit so moved.

ADVICE

Leave the dreaming
 to the dreamers.

The corporations
wish only your
obedience
and for this
they give you
what you suppose
is peace.

And you have
given your obedience
for so long
you can't tell
what you have lost

that your blood has
thinned and tainted

that you are a sickness

that canned laughter
and boxed expectations
seem normal now

endless war
normal now

your neighbor starving
normal now.

Leave the dreaming
to the dreamers.

You know they
are the lost ones
the foolish.

Not ever you.

You are in the know
intelligent and wise.

Your television
tells you this

and so it is true.

Leave the dreaming
to the dreamers.
Leave them to their work.

The dreamers
do not need you
as sad as that might be
and yes it truly is sad

as night takes hold
and we attend
our required pleasures

and the dreamers
dream.

RANT

Is there anything in this world better than good, under the skin, passionate conversation? Anything more intimate and pure? Conversation, of course, can be, should be, must be, more than words. Driving through the night in some old car, discovering another soul over greasy chicken and illicit beer as the miles stitch unimagined connections that become, in a flash, obvious and necessary. Eternal. Now, that's a conversation worth having. And the elements of the trip are one with all that is said. The night, the car, the chicken, the beer, the chosen road, the person in the seat beside you. Everything is one. Dear God, how delicious. Or quick banter with a pretty cashier at the grocery store. Or the fleeting wave from another driver as you let them into your lane on a crowded freeway. Even these can hold the fundamental balm of connection. Sex, of course, is conversation, that's obvious, spoken in the language of desire and conquest and need, one delicious line of discourse so primal it disrupts the boundaries of all other possible meanings. Conversation is life and is the animal foundation from which human character springs. I'm telling you this. I'm saying this to you now. It is inescapable and your sadness is filled with the absence of your reply.

Dear God. Talk. Talk. Listen. Talk. Gesture. Embrace. Laugh with me. Cry. This road is not forever. The beer and chicken won't last. Now is the time. Now is the chance. Know me. Know yourself. This is the only way. This is the world. It is all there ever has been and nothing, nothing, no spark can endure within a broken circuit. *Talk to me, baby.*

CONVERSATION WITH A FRIEND

She judged me for liking the Byrds
more than Dylan.
You know the type.
No?
Maybe that was what I liked about her,
the certainty that it even mattered.
If I say she radiated light,
will that make it more clear?
Jesus, what a cynic.
Haven't you ever been in love?
No?
Lucky you.
The thing is, I like Dylan.
Yes, even his voice.
Especially his voice.
Can you pass me that ashtray?
I want to give these things up, but it's so hard.
Look, we've known each other for a long time.
Can I tell you something?
It's just this: I hold a thing in my heart
that no one sees,
an obvious, fundamental thing

and I can't even say what it is.

Isn't that crazy?

Laugh if you want, but I need answers.

Why are we invisible,

when all we want is to be transparent?

Okay, fuck that. Can I drink this beer?

It's the last one, but I'll buy more.

The girl? I can't say she's gone

because she was never here to begin with.

And you know, the Byrds were a damned fine band.

LISTEN UP, PETTIGREW

trust the voice, Mr. Pettigrew
everything has value
the lies most of all

the voice can change everything
if you let it, Mr. Pettigrew

empires may rise and fall
love might escape betrayal
lives continue in the face of certain death

trust it

the voice comes from somewhere
the voice carries power

and here's the thing

the voice is your voice
Mr. Pettigrew
and, I say again
you should trust it

but trust is a hard-earned coin

the voice requires sacrifice
it requires work
and you are the laziest bastard drawing breath
Mr. Pettigrew

lie down in darkness
and find a comfortable spot
you're not going anywhere

A FEW CORONAS BEFORE LEAVING

Soft summer night of neighbors across the street
man laughter and woman laughter and children, oblivious,
riding through on bicycles big as dreams
—*Whatcha doin' Kelly?—Nothin'!*—
as though nothing existed but them and this moment
and what's more true than that?
Soft moist night hot with spiders
building castles on the porch, genius engineers
guided by nothing but ten million years of ancestors
—*yes, boy, good, spin out just a bit more, there!*—
as around the corner spins a lady on her bike,
no child she, nor spider, sensible reflector winking
red as she corners and, for the moment, is gone.
Darkness broken by life, impertinent and greedy,
twinkling under bashful heaven while I
read books and brood about Kerouac's fellaheen Mexico
two thousand miles south and west sinking soon
to its own dark night, and the lovely ladies, senoritas,
wondering what the other life is, never knowing
I was ever born, and I am drinking Coronas, a six pack with
number two half gone, Gwen gone with another, bless her,
she tried to fetch me to the party across the way. I bet you

can get this stuff on the cheap in Nogales Sonora or down
in the Yucatan or that nameless town where George drove
Pancho, toothless, footless, screaming *Tacate!*
at every billboard, barreling six hours down country to
brothers and sisters unseen for a decade,
who took in the travelers like they both were family.
Soft, soft night of no decision, soft aching night,
last chance night for adventure and that
great infinite starlit blanket casting
adoration forever and forever on the journey
and the journeyers. Soft night of pain and fear,
of shame and terror, of hope and no hope,
of making your own breaks and taking them where
you find them, of following where they lead.

EVENTUALLY, THERE IS NOTHING LEFT

Bright flashes of memory—
Wasn't there a girl, once?
A lace tablecloth?
Something about a cello?

Bother.

Here now, don't worry with that.

Matchstick men make matchstick lives.

No, of course not you.

Get along. Things are almost ready here.
Mind the rain. We don't need another tragedy.

What?

Yes, I thought she was delicate.
Who didn't in those days?

We all live with error and that

was mine. Now, we really must
say goodbye.

You've seen it, haven't you?
This empty room is less clever
than it supposes.

NIGHT WALK

It feels like the end of something,
no tomorrow
or a beginning in darkness.
Are these things different?
Such a still, cool night.
The world does not exist,
is everywhere around me.
Are these things different?
I almost know who I am.
I think so.
What is ending?
What can ever end in this false place?
Funhouse mirrors barely hint
At what we fail to see.

IT WAS MARGARET

She was a dancer
bathed in sweat
black hair surprised
with the leap and twist.

Tasteful nude photographs
paid the rent
and later
in her favorite café
the night brilliant
and chatting with friends
her thin fingers
aimlessly drumming
the sturdy table
she caught the eye
of a shy young man
who remembered her
to his final day.

Though he married
and fathered children

he was forever haunted
because he once saw love
across a crowded room
and never
knew her name.

THIS MOMENT WE HAVE

It is time for us to be good to one another.

Old women in the street begging money.
Children without food.
Vanished jobs
and life chances gone missing.
Skin and faith and accidents of birth.

Who we love.

It is time for us to be good to one another.

People taking to the streets.
Blank violence.
Refugees hated
because we need to hate someone.

Disbelief.
Fear of our neighbor.

It is time for us to be good to one another.

America confused or else gone crazy.

Hucksters lifted to power.

The fear of a knock at your door.

Open season on everyone who is different.

Everyone is different.

It is time for us to be good to one another.

Last chance to punch that ticket

before history does it for us.

It is time and time does not last.

Not in this world, my friends.

SMALL TALK AT THE
GREAT WATER COOLER
IN THE SKY

Inside the dream,

the dreamer lives

and so a world is made

and lit by wonders,

and beyond that world

is darkness

broken by small points of light

which the dreamer

believes to be titanic balls

of superheated gas,

known as "stars,"

but which are, of course,

the traces of our machine

gently pulling

the dreamer awake.

PLEASED TO MEET YOU

We inhabit these bodies.

We come from elsewhere
and live inside them
for a moment.

We inhabit moments
strung together
like popcorn.

We are dark magic
and vapor.

Anything else
is fairytale.

THIS FAMILY THAT WE ARE

Because dictators do this
and birds die like everything dies
and vision must work
through cracked windows
and smoke
and the statue
is only copper, steel, concrete, granite,
and hollow
because we are battered
and spat upon
because dictators do this
and dogs go hungry
and sometimes freeze
and children can only know
what they live
because the flag is ashes
and because the smiles
become gasps
become tears
become rage
become resolve
because we are the poor in spirit

and maybe blessed

because who will inherit anything

and who will stand in our way

and what comes crashing down

and when

is soon upon us

because the people

because the people

because the people

because we

stand up

because we fight

TOMORROW

When I awaken, perhaps the bakers
will give up on bread
and the firemen burn all the houses
and the children cease their play.
Maybe the rich will throw away gold
and birds crawl the earth
dogs bow down to cats
and all the lovely brides
escape to the forest.
Perhaps I will finally understand
how the tilt of the earth on its axis
is a love letter to the moon.

SARAH UNDERSTOOD

Sarah understood a lot of things.

She understood she had once mistaken
a darkness named Humphrey for romance.

She understood Humphrey drank too much vodka
and was hot for her sister.

She understood Humphrey had a sixth toe on his right foot
and she understood that this embarrassed him.

She understood that Humphrey sometimes beat her
because he was a miserable loser
who had to have someone to destroy.

She understood how to mix
rat poison
with hot and spicy chili
so you couldn't even taste it.

Sarah understood how to disappear.
She understood a lot.

LIKE EVERYONE

I need
real magic
a spell
an elixir
a fetish
a totem
dark powerful
goofer dust.

I need
an incantation
alchemy
peculiar solutions
from a
forgotten book.

I need to climb
impossible mountains
and dive into
lost waterfalls
swim miles
of open water

to escape
cannibal pirates.

I need to make
the art of ages
incandescent portraits
sculpture and poetry
pure creation
with lines sharp
as tigers' teeth.

I need a woman
to consume
and be
consumed by
a love
to make the world
and me
weep.

I need to hear her
whisper my name
just once
in a dark and silent room.

HEY, BROTHER

Hell is a
cold place
lacking
conversation
or I should say
it is all
locked doors
and silence.
Hell is what is left
when happiness dies
and you remain.
Hell is all the
good memories
turned sideways
and is ever
as close
as your
dearest ones
or in truth
as close as
your own skin.
Hell is

your destination
no matter what.
Welcome
to the club.

THE WAY

I have settled on a form
a single pattern
a way of focused intent
through stillness and movement

muscular tension and release

concentration of the will.

Proper stances are vital
and deceptively hard.

Every technique
should be perfect
and executed with intent
to kill the implacable air.

Age has given me
an evolved purpose.

Though I may look
weak to you

inside I am vast

a warrior.

I am the form
and will not yield.

REMIND ME HOW TO BE HUMAN

If you need my coat take it
my blood is already yours.

Bring out the hidden stones
and weigh them for their value.

Paint this moment in gray and black
but remember the joys of color.

Everything I have is given
and the wise will tell you
love is crazy starlight.

Prepare your heart
for the hollows.

They come so fast
and losing you
would kill me.

PRAISE THE LORD

Half-starved dog
on the church steps
like the poor man
seeking food
sleeps hungry
tonight
on the road
to nowhere
but tomorrow
is bingo night
and pot luck
come on neighbor
bring a friend.

ABSENT FRIEND

This one smoked Chesterfields
and sometimes quoted Yeats
when conversation fell awkward
and drummed her fingers on her leg
in the most fetching way.

She claimed to be an artist
and swore she had once been beautiful.

I cannot confirm
the geometries of her youth
but her eyes held more light than most
and she could throw back whiskey
like a sailor
and that was plenty for me.

Still, we mostly liked to sit on her porch
those long Sunday afternoons
and drink lemonade to wash down
the stories we stitched together
with what passed for joy

and now nothing matters
in that empty house
and I say that porch can burn

and flowers are a poor fare-thee-well
to one who will never see their beauty

and I have
in any case
forgotten about it all.

GOOD DAY

The mystery is revealed
by a child's necklace
hanging beneath
a framed photograph
of little girl
bathed in Christmas lights
this noon of lazy shadows
with a dog asleep on the couch
and the air finally cool
on my bare feet
and silence embracing the day
after such a very long time
of swelter.

HAPPY BIRTHDAY TO ME

Today I know all the words
but can't make them fit
a day to be unwell and take it straight on
a day underwater with Texas drowning
another day when New Orleans
awakens screaming
a day when I am just fifty-eight years old
and not a day more
a day when my stomach remains fat and soft
and my children appear to love me
old graybeard father with bad knees
and Jill still my sweetheart
twenty years past first blush
today I know all the words
but they are floating somewhere
out of reach or wedged under a rock
and nothing fits
the way it once seemed it might
but it is at last time for sleep
my little ones and darlings
and the hope that abides in dreams
and manifests in waking

good night to all and everything
good night.

THE INVESTIGATION IS ONGOING
YOU WILL BE INFORMED OF OUR PROGRESS

We understand
that creating art on demand
is as difficult as drowning a horse
and exactly as satisfying.

The investigation will determine your path.
The investigation will be your savior.

We know why you bleed and where.
All that remains is who did the cutting.

Now get that goddamned horse out of here.
You are running out of time.

YES, YOU

Right this second
and always
you are everywhere
in the space-time illusion
but being born
made you forget
just as it always does.
Wake up
you crazy god!

LET'S TWIST AGAIN

One day you awaken
and you're God
with light flooding
from your eyes
and fire blazing
in your fingers
your electric breath
bringing life
to what was dust.
Small stones
turn to flowers
and flowers
turn to stars
and stars
turn to your mirror
and you are
what you always were
still like everyone
like even the least among us
waiting for the necessary moment
to dance.

DO IT

The trick
to life
in the
whirlwind
is to
spin faster
than
the storm.

ENDLESSLY

We dream
all blank and hollow
of breathing fire
and bloody fights
and good whiskey after
we dream we dream
all blank and hollow
of young beauties
and bodies that still work
of lost friends
and the dead
and all the seas
never sailed
and every world
left undiscovered
all blank and hollow
we dream
we dream.

OH, LOST

Old Walt Whitman in forgotten vistas
old lost country
old Woody Guthrie on the wind
old Wobblies marching ghost streets
old promises
old loves who can't say your name
old keepsakes of misplaced faith
old men alone
old women clutching final coins
old days in small rooms
old, unspoken dreams
old embrace of the dead
old people who loved
now turned to dust
and you,
old traveler, the last mystery,
even now
you should be dancing.

FREUD VISITS THE TROPICS

Sometimes
a cigar
is just
a banana.

IN CASE YOU DIDN'T KNOW

The poem will kill you if you let it.
The poem wants to come into the
world any way it can,
and that certainly means
at your expense;
at the expense of your sleep,
at the expense of your job,
your marriage,
your sanity.
The poem will kill you being born,
or worse, it will remain inside you,
hidden like a disease you sense
but can't name,
and no one else has any notion
of its existence,
while it grows,
spreads,
metastasizes.
The poem has no conscience,
though it is pure soul,
soul stolen right from your center.
The poem is a sorry bastard,

your best friend,

your life eternal,

and your damnation.

The poem is brutal,

and make no mistake,

I'm talking

straight as I know how,

straight as I can.

I mean this poem,

right now,

and the next one

you write,

and everything else

that stirs and bites

at your insides,

as the people

walk their dogs,

and the lonesome and cruel

cruise anonymous streets

in dangerous rides,

and love remains empty,

and poverty crushes the aged,

and maidens turn away,

and the world spins hotter,

and children grow old,
and all the dreams
awaken to silence.
This poem will kill you.
Think of it as mercy;
think of it as inevitable;
think of it as your reward,
as you slip into feeble skin
and are forgotten,
even by your own.
Maybe that will help.

WHY CAN'T YOU UNDERSTAND?

Everyone is almost beautiful
and adorned with beads
in the room where a cat
you do not know
is a spirit animal
not yours but someone's
and you love fiercely
both the cat and the people
while the beads
golden and blue
sparkle like incognito stars
and adorn the men and women
as the cat yawns
and purrs epic stories
you are too dull to grasp
and almost beautiful women
laugh at jokes
told by God at your expense
as the cat wanders off
leaving you shaken and alone
hideous
delighted

and driven to ground
amid this cyphered
and dying
glory.

SOMETHING

There is something
in deep space
that appears be
a craft
from another star
and there is something
in the White House
with orders
from Russia
and there is something
in my heart
that cuts deep and hard
and there is something
in your eyes
I cannot do without
and there is something
beyond understanding
that I sometimes almost get
and there is something
in the wind
that will come
no matter what

and there is something
in this world
that will be the last thing
we will ever share
and there is something
heading this way
that will finally end us
but that will not
my dear
be tonight.

NIXON VS. THE FLYING SAUCERS

He'd only been in office
a few months when Nixon began
hearing the voices.
"We are from Voltan," they said
whispering to him in the night.
He was afraid to tell anyone
even Pat.
Nobody noticed anything strange
until one day the President
came to a cabinet meeting
dressed all in silver
a big glass bubble on his head.
It was all Mitchell could do
to wrestle him to the carpet
before he pulled a gun
straight out of Buck Rogers
screaming *Take me to your leader!*"
The next day
a new man was installed in office
a double
and nobody was ever the wiser
and now Nixon lives in a cage

at Fort Bragg, N.C.
Sometimes the Voltanians
still speak to him
and even offer dangerous plans for escape
but usually they just lay back and giggle
cruising the galaxy
and looking for kicks.

HOMELESS NIXON

Nixon offered to stay on
at the White House
as Ford's valet or cook
but it was no dice.

"*Get out, you leech!*" screamed Gerry
tossing Dick and Pat's suitcases
into the Rose Garden.
"Tough titty if you didn't
plan for retirement."

Now you can sometimes
catch a glimpse
of the former first couple
on the streets of D.C.
foraging for food
or rolling tourists.

Nixon's lost some weight
but his eyes shine dark dark dark.
They say he's planning a comeback
if only he can

put together a bankroll
one quarter at a time.
"Hey, mister," he says.
"Mister? Spare change for the old?
For the forgotten?
Hey, mister?
I used to be
somebody...."

KEROUAC ELVIS

Neal was so bummed
by the universal
conspiracy of
cosmic reality
bombarding his
moments of illusory
timespace with
negative vibratory
emanations that as
he rolled a jay
with one hand
and Elvis passed
him a beer he
almost failed
to negotiate a
hairpin turn on
that mountain
pass just south
of Guaymas, Mexico –
The King just sat there
examining his ducktail
in the rearview

muttering something
about Burroughs
and yage
his hands twitching
toward the window
the wind
and the lovely
Mexican night

WASN'T SIDNEY POITIER IN THAT?

consider the

c

o

  n

   s

    i

     d

      e

       r   the

lilies

    lilies

of

   the

field

     consider

   the lilies

   consider the lilies

      consider

      consider

        the

          field

TIME WITH THE DOG

On the stairs
with the dog
as the cat lurks
in silence
and the moon
tiptoes
across the sky
and my children
dream their dreams
and the world
spins on
for now.

On the stairs
with the dog
as my wife reads
a book
behind a closed door
and my children dream
and the moon
moves on
and people

up and down

my street

live unknown

lives.

On the stairs

with the dog

as the cat

plots our deaths

and darkness comes

and the neighbors

are all ghosts

and my children

dream

and my wife

reads her book

and the world

spins on

for now.

EVEN THE FORTUNATE

Some think of Dylan Thomas and some think of the dead
and some think of birds flown south and some think of lost
nights on barstools and some think of the rings of Saturn
and some think of unknown worlds and some think of
cancer and children and some think of darkness falling and
some think of you in your weary confusion and some think
of masterpieces on museum walls and some think of clean
houses and plenty and some think of sea turtles and some
think of Christ's acquiescence and some think of painless
dentistry and some think of good dogs and some think of
things you will never imagine.

Some think there is a way home
but everything kills us just the same.

CRUISE

gritty stars glow white
as cars smooth down lake drive
16-year-old girls giggling beer
onto t-shirts
tail lights flashing danger
like rattles glowing with blood
and promise
boys hang tough in parking lots
cigarettes suspended from sneers
tattoo dreams
sliding through uncounted moments
separated by desire
while night washes through their fingers
like water

SO IT GOES

Dead leaves
beneath the wheels
of bicycles
ridden by old men
on Tuscaloosa streets
while young women
think of other things.

ALCHEMY OF THE PAGE

Most unsavory, turning your friends into minor characters,
into heroes and fiends in those novels you carried in that
rucksack, nobody interested, and you drunk again on port
or Benzedrine flying. The least you could do was give them
good aliases.

I mean, come on – Japhy Rider?
Adam Moorad?
Mardou Fox?

And you wondered why Neal walked away hurt the day you
christened him to the world as psychopathic Dean
Moriarty and that was almost that.

How strange.

Of all that madness, all that remains is ink and yellow
paper and the ineptitude of our various blurred visions.

PROF

She said she cried
when she saw the draft
of his poem
in pencil
on regular paper

because now

during her dissertation research

she had at last
discovered
poems were written
by real people
with real lives

a golf game that day
and the poem vanishes.

I envied her outburst
realizing
what I'd known

for a long while
about English teachers.

And though I knew
there was nothing
I could do
I shrunk inside

thinking

"Is this what
I have come to

is this where I am going?"

IF YOU HAVE THE COURAGE

Ask the dust on the bones
of dead writers
and yellowed paper cluttered
with courier sentences
no one ever saw.
Ask the road to Los Angeles
and the carcasses of dead animals
strewn beneath the beating sun.
Ask the sheltering sky.
Ask the brethren of late night terror
of blank pages
and untouched keys.
Ask the blood of the grape.
Ask the dust of your dreams.
Ask the readers who never arrive.
Ask tomorrow who you were
and the answer is nothing.
The answer is nothing,
or not even that.
The answer is fool.
Ask the men in suits.
Ask the beautiful women.

Ask the grocer with his plenty.
Ask Fante on your shelf.
Ask the love that never was.
Ask the forgotten blessings
and find what peace you may
in your own hot blood.
Deliver what you can.
That is all.

WRITER'S BLOCK

Ever notice
how there's

never a good
red wheelbarrow

around when
you need one?

GO THE DISTANCE

Write a boxing story in Hemingway's style.

Make it in the dressing room
just after the fight
or in the tunnel heading
to the ring.

Make it about
a fighter who may have won
or may have lost.

Make it about the death of love
or the ruin of a loved one,
a child perhaps.

Or make it about the fighter's
cheating wife.

Write a story where everything
depends on incidental detail.
Write it true and pure.
Write it like a beating.

Write it like blood.
Write it like all the times
you had to win and still lost
but didn't quit.

Write it like Papa taught you.

That's the only heaven there is,
the only hope.

Write the story like Hemingway
like Fitzgerald
like Bukowski
like Faulker.

Write it like Barry Hannah or Erskine Caldwell.
Like Flannery O'Connor or Harper Lee.

Write it like any of the giants of before.
Only better.

They have nothing on you.

Write it the way nobody ever could

before this moment
before you came along
with that swagger
that murderous need
that moxie.

Come out swinging
while you still have a chance.
Never mind the possibility of
despair, of anguish
of wrong words
or no words.

Accept the defeats
that will surely come
the beatings, the cuts,
the humiliations
of poverty and need
or the apathy of publishers.

These things do not matter
except to make you ready,
make you strong.
You're in it for the distance

not fame, not money,
not yielding flesh,
though sometimes these come
incidentally to the victor.

You have your eye on the belt
and the belt is the story
the novel
the poem

the best thing you alone can do.

Take the chance
because chances become
more rare by the hour
and the hours are swift.

This is the way
and there is no other.

Papa knew.
They all did.

Your turn, champ.

FIGHTERS

The kid was lightning fast
but didn't get his body into it
so there was nothing
on his punches
but sweat and air.

Still, the ladies loved him
and he climbed the rankings fast
out-pointing one bum
after another
and at 15-0 got a title shot.

The champ was a couple of years
past his prime
but knew how to hit
the way a fighter should
with everything working together
from the soles of his feet
to the hard bones of his knuckles.

The trendy money was on the kid
and the fight went his way

as he danced and flicked his hands
to the middle of the eighth
when the champ finally landed
a hook to the ribs
that almost killed him
and ended it with a straight right
to the jaw.

The kid was never right after that
and started losing matches
he would have easily won before.

Pretty soon the big fights
didn't come his way
and, after the money was gone,
so were the women.

The champ lost his next
and settled into a sad retirement

while the kid hit the bars
with his stories of the glory days
and how he'd have the belt right now
without those lucky punches.

They're both dead now, of course,
and buried in this boneyard.

It takes a little work
to find the kid's stone,
tasteful and untouched,
blending seamlessly
with the others,

but the champ is easy.

You'll find his grave
in that far corner
away from everyone.

It's the one with all the flowers.

PUNCHER'S CHANCE

The fight is yours
for the shortest moment
just as it once
belonged to others
and will soon enough
belong to someone else.

Cherish the battle
until you are truly beaten.

Someday the fight will devour you
but this is your moment of grace.

Don't be stupid.

You can't win
but, as the wise old woman in the dark
will tell you,
everything is worth it.

About the Author

Jeff Weddle grew up in Prestonsburg, a small town in the hill country of eastern Kentucky. He has worked as a public library director, disc jockey, newspaper reporter, Tae Kwon Do teacher, and fry cook, among other things. His first book, *Bohemian New Orleans: The Story of the Outsider and Loujon Press* (University Press of Mississippi, 2007), won the Eudora Welty Prize and helped inspire Wayne Ewing's documentary, *The Outsiders of New Orleans: Loujon Press* (Wayne Ewing Films, 2007). He teaches in the School of Library and Information Studies at the University of Alabama.

About the Publisher

Rust Belt Press was conceived in early 2019 based on the desire to promote the small press world and its many talented avant-garde writers and artists.

Rust Belt Press currently has titles available by Robert Keith, Ryan Quinn Flanagan, and Jeff Weddle with forthcoming projects by Matthew Borczon and others.

The bimonthly periodical, *Rust Belt Review*, was launched in January 2019.

Rust Belt Press may currently be found on Facebook, Twitter, Instagram, and YouTube.

Email - rustbeltpressandreview@gmail.com

Website – https://rustbeltpress.net

Lulustore -

http://www.lulu.com/spotlight/Rust_Belt_Press

www.ingramcontent.com/pod-product-compliance
Lightning Source LLC
Chambersburg PA
CBHW051828040426
42447CB00006B/429